Hippocrene
CHILDREN'S
ILLUSTRATED
RUSSIAN
DICTIONARY

ENGLISH · RUSSIAN
RUSSIAN · ENGLISH

Compiled and translated by the Editors of Hippocrene Books

Interior illustrations by S. Grant (24, 81, 88); J. Gress (page 10, 21, 24, 37, 46, 54, 59, 65, 72, 75, 77);
K. Migliorelli (page 13, 14, 18, 19, 20, 21, 22, 25, 31, 32, 37, 39, 40, 46, 47, 66, 71, 75, 76, 82, 86, 87);
B. Swidzinska (page 9, 11, 12, 13, 14, 16, 23, 27, 28, 30, 32, 33, 35, 37, 38, 41, 42, 45, 46, 47, 48, 49, 50,
52, 53, 56, 57, 58, 59, 60, 61, 62, 63, 66, 68, 69, 70, 71, 72, 73, 75, 77, 78, 79, 83), N. Zhukov (page 8, 13,
14, 17, 18, 23, 27, 29, 33, 34, 39, 40, 41, 52, 64, 65, 71, 72, 73, 78, 84, 86, 88).

Design, prepress, and production: Graafiset International, Inc.

Cataloging-in-Publication Data available from the Library of Congress.

ISBN 0-7818-0772-7

Printed in Hong Kong

For information, address:
Hippocrene Books, Inc.
171 Madison Avenue
New York, NY 10016

INTRODUCTION

With their absorbent minds, infinite curiosities and excellent memories, children have enormous capacities to master many languages. All they need is exposure and encouragement.

The easiest way to learn a foreign language is to simulate the same natural method by which a child learns English. The natural technique is built on the concept that language is representational of concrete objects and ideas. The use of pictures and words are the natural way for children to begin to acquire a new language.

The concept of this Illustrated Dictionary is to allow children to build vocabulary and initial competency naturally. Looking at the pictorial content of the Dictionary and saying and matching the words in connection to the drawings gives children the opportunity to discover the foreign language and thus, a new way to communicate.

The drawings in the Dictionary are designed to capture children's imaginations and make the learning process interesting and entertaining, as children return to a word and picture repeatedly until they begin to recognize it.

The beautiful images and clear presentation make this dictionary a wonderful tool for unlocking your child's multilingual potential.

Deborah Dumont, M.A., M.Ed.,
Child Psychologist and Educational Consultant

РУССКИЙ АЛФАВИТ

RUSSIAN ALPHABET

Аа	Кк	Хх
Бб	Лл	Цц
Вв	Мм	Чч
Гг	Нн	Шш
Дд	Оо	Щщ
Ее	Пп	Ъъ
Ёё	Рр	Ыы
Жж	Сс	Ьь
Зз	Тт	Зз
Ии	Уу	Юю
Йй	Фф	Яя

RUSSIAN PRONUNCIATION

Letters	Pronunciation system used	
а	**a**	as in 'father' but short
а	**aa**	as in 'car' (long)
ай	**oy**	like *ye* in 'bye'
г	**g**	as in 'garden'
е	**ye**	as in 'yes' (at the beginning of a word)
ё	**yo**	as in 'yolk' (at the beginning of a word)
ей	**ey**	as in 'hey'
ж	**zh**	like the *s* in 'leisure'
з	**z**	as in 'zebra'
и	**i**	as in 'eel' but short
	ee	as in 'see' when long
й	**y**	as in 'kayak'
о	**o**	as in 'omit' when short
	oh	as in 'door' when long
р	**r**	as in 'burro' (trilled as in Spanish)
с	**s**	as in 'salt'
у	**oo**	as in 'tooth'
х	**kh**	like the *ch* in Scottish 'loch'
ц	**ts**	as in 'cats'
ч	**ch**	as in 'cherry'
ш	**sh**	as in 'ship'
щ	**shch**	as in 'fresh cheese'
ь	**"**	at the end of a syllable softens the preceding consonant
ы	**y**	like the *i* in 'big'
э	**eh**	like the *e* in 'elbow'
ю	**yu**	like the *you* in 'youth'
я	**ya**	as in 'yard'

ъ   at the end of a syllable: short pause, as between words

(i)   softens the preceding consonant: press the tongue to the palate while pronouncing the consonant, for example   sa-mo-l(i)ot.

'   Apostrophy before a syllable indicates that this syllable is stressed

airplane   самолёт
sa-mo-'l(i)ot

alligator   аллигатор
al-l(i)i-'ga-tor

alphabet   алфавит
al-fa-'vit

antelope   антилопа
an-ti-'lo-pa

antlers   оленьи рога
o-l(i)'en"-ee ro-'ga

apple   яблоко
'yab-lo-ko

aquarium   аквариум
ak-'va-r(i)i-oom

arch   арка
'ar-ka

arrow   стрела
str(i)e-'la

autumn   осень
'o-s(i)en"

baby   младенец
mla-'d(i)e-n(i)ets

backpack   рюкзак
r(i)uk-'zak

badger   барсук
bar-'sook

baker   пекарь
'p(i)e-kar''

ball   мяч
m(i)ach

balloon   воздушный шар
voz-'doosh-ny shar

banana банан
ba-'nan

barley ячмень
yach-'men"

barrel бочка
'boch-ka

basket корзинка
kor-'z(i)i-nka

bat летучая мышь
l(i)e-'too-cha-ya mysh

beach пляж
pl(i)azh

bear медведь
m(i)ed-'v(i)ed"

beaver бобр
bo-'br

bed кровать
kro-'vat"

bee пчела
pche-'la

beetle жук
zhook

bell колокол
'ko-lo-kol

belt   пояс
'po-yas

bench   скамья
skam-'ya

bicycle   велосипед
v(i)e-lo-si-'p(i)ed

binoculars   бинокль
bi-'nokl"

bird   птица
'pti-tsa

birdcage   птичья клетка
'pt(i)i-chya 'kl(i)et-ka

black чёрный
'chyor-ny

blocks кубики
'koo-bi-ki

blossom цвет
tsv(i)et

blue синий
'see-n(i)y

boat лодка
'lod-ka

bone кость
kost"

book   книга
'kn(i)i-ga

boot   сапог
sa-'pog

bottle   бутылка
boo-'tyl-ka

bowl   миска
'm(i)is-ka

boy   мальчик
'mal''-chik

bracelet   браслет
bras-'l(i)et

branch
ветка
'v(i)et-ka

bread
хлеб
khl(i)eb

breakfast
завтрак
'zav-trak

bridge
мост
most

broom
метла
m(i)et-'la

brother
брат
braat

brown   коричневый
ko-'rich-n(i)e-vy

brush   щётка
'shchyot-ka

bucket   ведро
v(i)ed-'ro

bulletin board доска объявлений
dos-'ka 'ob'-yav-l(i)e-n(i)y

bumblebee   шмель
shm(i)el"

butterfly   бабочка
'ba-boch-ka

cab

такси
tak-'s(i)i

cabbage

капуста
ka-'poos-ta

cactus

кактус
'kak-toos

café

кафэ
ka-'feh

cake

торт
tort

camel

верблюд
v(i)er-'bl(i)ood

C

camera фотоаппарат
fo-to-ap-pa-'rat

candle свечка
'sv(i)ech-ka

candy конфета
kon-'f(i)e-ta

canoe байдарка
bay-'dar-ka

cap шапка
'shap-ka

captain капитан
ka-p(i)i-'tan

car   автомобиль

af-to-mo-'bil"

card   карта

'kaar-ta

carpet   ковер

ko-'v(i)or

carrot   морковь

mor-'kov"

(to) carry   нести

n(i)es-t(i)i

castle   замок

'zaa-mok

cat   кошка
'kosh-ka

cave   пещера
p(i)esh-'che-ra

chair   стул
stool

cheese   сыр
syr

cherry   черешня
che-'r(i)esh-nya

chimney   труба
troo-'ba

chocolate шоколад
sho-ko'lad

Christmas tree ёлка
'yol-ka

circus цирк
tsyrk

(to) climb лазить
'laa-zit"

cloud облако
'ob-la-ko

clown клоун
'klo-oon

coach карета
ka-'r(i)e-ta

coat пальто
pal"-'to

coconut кокос
ko-'kos

comb расчёска
ras-'chyos-ka

comforter одеяло
o-d(i)e-'ya-lo

compass компас
'kom-pas

(to) cook   варить
va-'rit"

cork   пробка
'prob-ka

corn   кукуруза
koo-koo-'roo-za

cow   корова
ko-'ro-va

cracker   печенье
pe'che-nye

cradle   колыбель
ko-ly-'bel"

(to) crawl ползать
'pol-zat''

(to) cross переходить
p(i)e-r(i)e-kho-'d(i)it''

crown корона
ko-'ro-na

(to) cry плакать
'pla-kat''

cucumber огурец
ogoo-'r(i)ets

curtain занавеска
za-na-'v(i)es-ka

(to) dance   танцевать
tan-tse-'vat"

dandelion   одуванчик
o-doo-'van-chik

date   число
'chis-'lo

deer   олень
o-'len"

desert   пустыня
poos-'ty-n(i)a

desk   парта
'par-ta

dirty   грязный
'gr(i)az-nyy

dog   собака
                           so-'ba-ka

doghouse   конура
                           ko-noo-'ra

doll   кукла
                           'kook-la

dollhouse   игрушечный домик
                 ig-'roo-shech-ny 'do-mik

dolphin   дельфин
                           'del"-fin

donkey   осёл
                           o-'s(i)ol

dragon   дракон
                           dra-'kon

dragonfly   стрекоза
str(i)e-ko-'za

(to) draw   рисовать
ri-so-'vat"

dress   платье
'plat"-ye

(to) drink   пить
pit"

drum   барабан
ba-ra-'ban

duck   утка
'oot-ka

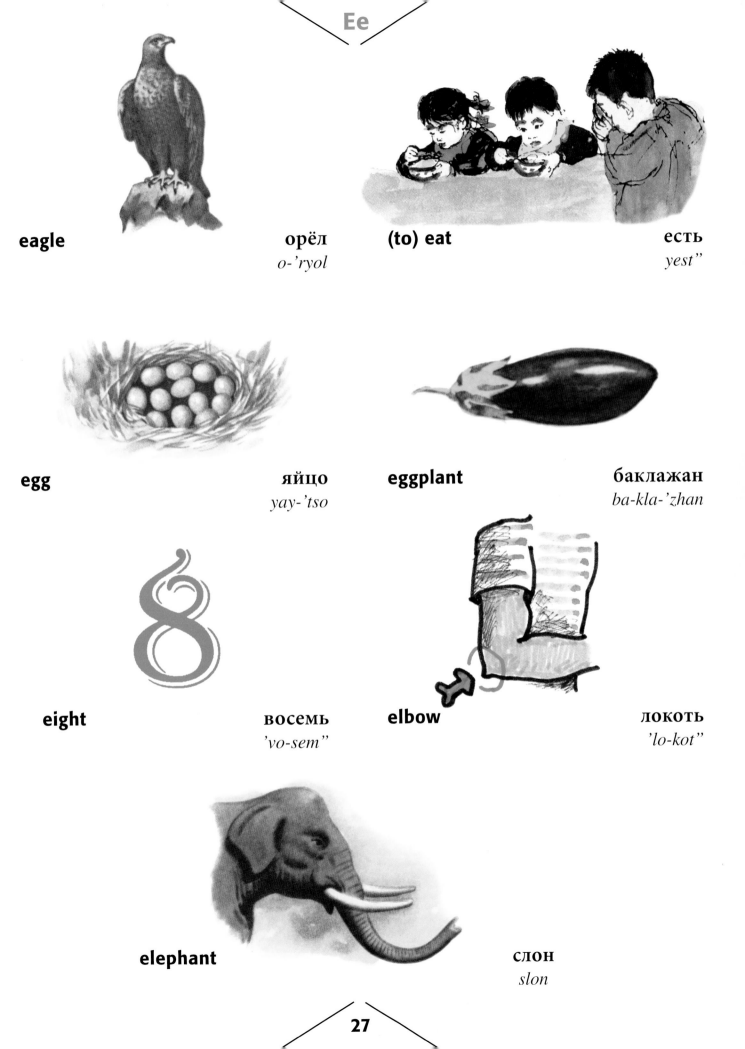

eagle   орёл
o-'ryol

(to) eat   есть
yest"

egg   яйцо
yay-'tso

eggplant   баклажан
ba-kla-'zhan

eight   восемь
'vo-sem"

elbow   локоть
'lo-kot"

elephant   слон
slon

empty   пустой
poos-'toy

engine   паровоз
pa-ro-'voz

envelope   конверт
kon-'v(i)ert

escalator   эскалатор
es-ka-'la-tor

Eskimo   эскимос
ehs-ki-'mos

(to) explore   исследовать
is-'sl(i)e-do-vat''

eye   глаз
glaz

face   лицо
l(i)i-'tso

fan   вентилятор
ven-t(i)i-'l(i)a-tor

father   отец
o-'t(i)ets

fear   страх
strakh

feather   перо
p(i)e-'ro

(to) feed   кормить
kor-'m(i)it"

fence　　　　　забор
　　　　　　　　　za-'bor

fern　　　　　папоротник
　　　　　　　　　'pa-po-rot-n(i)ik

field　　　　　поле
　　　　　　　　　'po-l(i)e

field mouse　　полевая мышь
　　　　　　　　　po-l(i)e-'va-ya mysh

finger　　　　　палец
　　　　　　　　　'pa-l(i)ets

fir tree　　　　ель
　　　　　　　　　yel"

fire огонь
o-'gon"

fish рыба
'ry-ba

(to) fish удить
oo-'d(i)it"

fist кулак
koo-'lak

five пять
'p(i)at"

flag флаг
flaag

flashlight   фонарик
fo-'na-rik

(to) float держаться на поверхности
dyer'-zhatsya na po'-verkhno-sti

flower   цветок
tsv(i)e-'tok

(to) fly   летать
l(i)e-tat"

foot   нога
no-'ga

fork   вилка
'v(i)il-ka

fountain   фонтан
fon-'tan

four четыре
che-'ty-r(i)e

fox лиса
l(i)i-'sa

frame рама
'ra-ma

friend друг
droog

frog лягушка
l(i)a-'goosh-ka

fruit фрукты
'frook-ty

furniture мебель
'm(i)e-bel"

garden сад
sad

gate ворота
vo'-ro-ta

(to) gather собирать
so-b(i)i-rat"

geranium герань
g(i)e-'ran"

giraffe жираф
zhi-'raf

girl девочка
d(i)e-voch-ka

(to) give   давать
da-'vat"

glass   стакан
sta-'kan

glasses   очки
och-'kee

globe   глобус
'glo-boos

glove   перчатка
p(i)er-'chat-ka

goat   коза
ko-'za

goldfish   золотая рыбка
zo-lo-'ta-ya   'ryb-ka

"Good Night" **"Спокойной ночи"**
spo-'koy-noy   'no-chi

"Good-bye"   **"До свидания"**
do svi-'da-n(i)ya

goose   гусь
goos"

grandfather   дедушка
'd(i)e-doosh-ka

grandmother   бабушка
'ba-boosh-ka

grapes   виноград
v(i)i-no-'grad

grasshopper   кузнечик
kooz-'n(i)e-chik

green   зеленый
z(i)e-'l(i)o-nyy

greenhouse   парник
par-'n(i)ik

guitar   гитара
g(i)i-'ta-ra

hammer

молоток

mo-lo-'tok

hammock

гамак

ga-'mak

hamster

хомяк

kho-'m(i)ak

hand

рука

roo-'ka

handbag

сумка

'soom-ka

handkerchief

платочек

pla-'to-chek

harvest   урожай
oo-ro-'zhay

hat   шляпа
'shl(i)a-pa

hay   сено
's(i)e-no

headdress   головной убор
go-lov-'noy oo-'bor

heart   сердце
's(i)er-tse

hedgehog   ёж
yozh

hen курица
'koo-r(i)i-tsa

(to) hide прятаться
'pr(i)a-tat"-s(i)a

highway шоссе
shos-'seh

honey мёд
m(i)od

horns рога
ro-'ga

horse конь
kon"

horseshoe   подкова
pod-'ko-va

hourglass   песочные часы
pe-'soch-ny-ye cha-'sy

house   дом
dom

(to) hug   обнимать
ob-n(i)i-'mat"

hydrant   пожарная колонка
po-'zhar-naya ko-'lon-ka

ice cream   мороженое
mo-'ro-zhe-no-ye

ice cubes   кубики льда
'koo-bi-ki l''da

ice-skating   кататься на коньках
ka-'tat-s(i)a na kon''-'kakh

instrument   инструмент
in-stroo-'m(i)ent

iris   ирис
'ee-r(i)is

iron   утюг
oo-'tyug

island   остров
'os-trov

jacket пиджак
pid-'zhaak

jam джем
dzhehm

jigsaw puzzle складная картинка
sklad-'na-ya kar-'t(i)in-ka

jockey жокей
zho-'key

juggler жонглёр
zhon-'gl(i)or

(to) jump скакать
ska-'kat"

kangaroo   кенгуру
k(i)en-goo-'roo

key   ключ
kl(i)ooch

kitten   котёнок
ko-'t(i)o-nok

knife   нож
nozh

knight   рыцарь
'ry-tsar"

(to) knit   вязать на спицах
v(i)a-'zat" na sp(i)i-'tsakh

knot   узел
'oo-z(i)el

koala bear   коала
ko-'a-la

ladder   лестница
'l(i)est-n(i)i-tsa

ladybug   божья коровка
'bozh-ya ko'rov-ka

lamb   барашек
ba-'ra-shek

lamp   лампа
'lam-pa

(to) lap   лакать
la-'kat''

laughter   смех
sm(i)ekh

lavender   лаванда
la-'van-da

lawn mower   косилка
ko-'s(i)il-ka

leaf   лист
l(i)ist

leg   нога
no-'ga

lemon   лимон
l(i)i-'mon

lettuce   салат
sa-'lat

lightbulb   лампочка
'lam-poch-ka

lighthouse   маяк
ma-'yak

lilac   сирень
s(i)i-'ren"

lion   лев
l(i)ev

(to) listen   слушать
'sloo-shat"

lobster   омар
o-'mar

lock замок
za-'mok

lovebird канарейка
ka-na-'r(i)ey-ka

luggage багаж
ba-'gazh

lumberjack лесоруб
l(i)e-so-'roob

lunch обед
o-'b(i)ed

lynx рысь
rys"

magazine   журнал
zhoor-'nal

magician   фокусник
'fo-koos-nik

magnet   магнит
mag-'n(i)it

map   карта
'kar-ta

maple leaf   кленовый лист
kl(i)e-'no-vy l(i)ist

marketplace   рынок
'ry-nok

mask   маска
'mas-ka

messy **беспорядок**
b(i)es-po-'r(i)a-dok

milkman **молочник**
mo-'loch-nik

mirror **зеркало**
'z(i)er-ka-lo

mitten **рукавица**
roo-ka-'v(i)i-tsa

money **деньги**
'd(i)en"-gi

monkey **обезьяна**
o-b(i)ez-'ya-na

moon **луна**
loo-'na

mother   мать
mat"

mountain   гора
go-'ra

mouse   мышь
mysh

mouth   рот
roht

mushroom   гриб
gr(i)ib

music   музыка
'moo-zy-ka

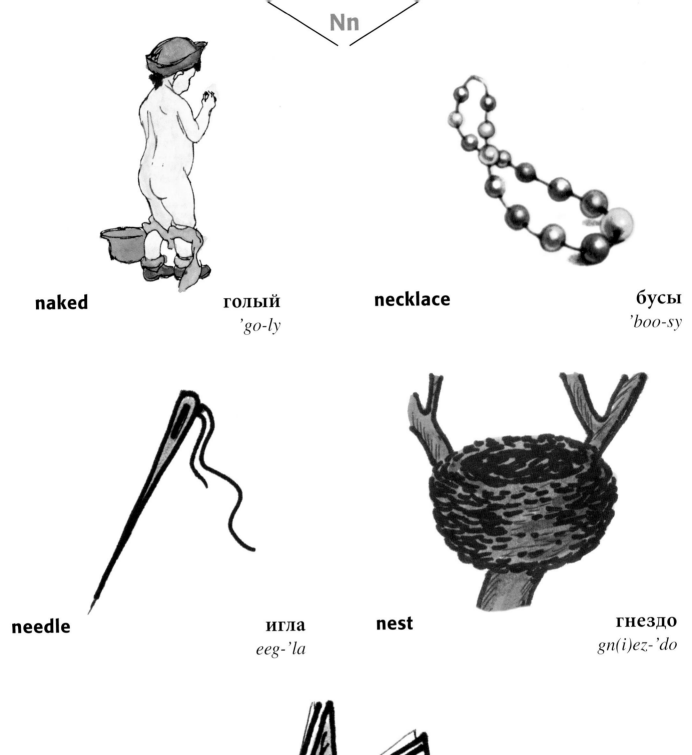

naked голый
'go-ly

necklace бусы
'boo-sy

needle игла
eeg-'la

nest гнездо
gn(i)ez-'do

newspaper газета
ga-'z(i)e-ta

nightingale　　соловей　　　　**nine**　　девять
so-lo-'v(i)ey　　　　　　　　　　　*d(i)e-'v(i)at"*

notebook　　тетрадь　　　　**number**　　число
t(i)et-'rad"　　　　　　　　　　　*ch(i)is-'lo*

nut　　　　　　　　　　　орех
o-r(i)ekh

oar весло
v(i)es-'lo

ocean liner океанский лайнер
ok(i)e-'an-sk(i)iy 'lay-ner

old старый
'sta-ry

one один
o-'d(i)in

onion лук
look

open открыто
ot-'kry-to

orange апельсин
a-p(i)el"-'s(i)in

ostrich страус
'stra-oos

owl сова
so-'va

ox бык
byk

padlock замок
za-'tok

paint краска
'kras-ka

painter художник
khoo-'dozh-n(i)ik

pajamas пижама
p(i)i-'zha-ma

palm tree пальма
'pal"-ma

paper бумага
boo-'ma-ga

parachute парашют
pa-ra-'shoot

park

парк
park

parrot

попугай
po-poo-'gay

passport

паспорт
'pas-port

patch

заплата
zap-'la-ta

path

дорожка
do-'rozh-ka

peach

персик
'p(i)er-s(i)ik

pear

груша
'groo-sha

pebble

галька
'gal''ka

(to) peck

клевать
kl(i)e-'vat''

(to) peel

чистить
'ch(i)is-t(i)it''

pelican

пеликан
p(i)e-l(i)i-'kan

pencil

карандаш
ka-ran-'dash

penguin

пингвин
p(i)in-'gv(i)in

people

люди
'l(i)oo-d(i)i

piano   пианино
p(i)i-a-'n(i)i-no

pickle   маринованный огурец
ma-ri-no'-va-nnyy o-goo-'rets

pie   пирог
p(i)i-'rog

pig   свинья
sv(i)in"-'ya

pigeon   голубь
'go-loob"

pillow   подушка
po-'doosh-ka

pin   булавка
boo-'lav-ka

pine   сосна
sos-'na

pineapple   ананас
a-na-'nas

pit   косточка
'kos-toch-ka

pitcher   кувшин
koov-'shin

plate   тарелка
ta-'r(i)el-ka

platypus   утконос
oot-ko-'nos

(to) play   играть
ig-'rat"

plum   слива
sl(i)i-'va

polar bear   белый медведь
b(i)e-ly m(i)ed-v(i)ed"

pony   пони
'po-n(i)i

pot   кастрюля
kas'-tryu-lya

potato   картофель
kar-'to-f(i)el"

(to) pour   наливать
na-l(i)i-'vat"

present   подарок
po-'dar-ok

(to) pull   тянуть
t(i)a-'noot"

pumpkin   тыква
'tyk-va

Qq

puppy   щенок
shche-'nok

queen   королева
ko-ro-'l(i)e-va

rabbit

кролик
'kro-l(i)ik

raccoon

енот
ye-'not

racket

ракетка
ra-'k(i)et-ka

radio

радио
'ra-d(i)i-o

radish

редиска
r(i)e-'d(i)is-ka

raft надувной плот
na-doov-'noy plot

rain дождь
dozhd"

rainbow радуга
'ra-doo-ga

raincoat дождевик
dozh-d(i)e-'v(i)ik

raspberry малина
ma-'l(i)i-na

(to) read читать
chi-'tat''

red красный
'kras-ny

refrigerator холодильник
kho-lo-'d(i)l''nik

rhinoceros носорог
no-so-'rog

ring кольцо
kol''-'tso

(to) ring   звонить
zvo-'nit''

river   река
re-'ka

road   дорога
do-'ro-ga

rocket   ракета
ra-'k(i)e-ta

roof   крыша
'kry-sha

rooster   петух
p(i)e-'tookh

root   корень
ko'-ren"

rope   канат
ka-'nat

rose   роза
'ro-za

(to) row   грести
gres-'ti

ruler   линейка
li-n(i)ey-ka

(to) run   бежать
be-'zhat"

safety pin английская булавка
an-gl(i)iy-ska-ya boo-'lav-ka

(to) sail ходить под парусом
kho-'d(i)it" pod 'paa-roo-som

sailor матрос
mat-'ros

salt соль
sol"

scarf шарф
sharf

school школа
'shko-la

scissors   ножницы
'nozh-n(i)i-tsy

screwdriver   отвёртка
ot-'v(i)ort-ka

seagull   чайка
'chay-ka

seesaw   качание на доске
ka-'cha-n(i)ye na dos-'k(i)e

seven   семь
sem"

(to) sew   шить
sheet"

shark   акула
a-'koo-la

sheep   овца
ov-'tsa

shell   ракушка
ra-'koosh-ka

shepherd   пастух
pas-'tookh

ship   корабль
ko-'raabl"

shirt   рубашка
roo-'bash-ka

shoe   ботинок
bo-t(i)i-nok

shovel   лопата
lo-'paa-ta

(to) show   показывать
po-'ka-zy-vat"

shower   душ
doosh

shutter   ставень
'sta-ven"

sick   больной
bol"-'noy

sieve   сито
'see-to

(to) sing   петь
p(i)et"

(to) sit   сидеть
s(i)i-'d(i)et"

six   шесть
shest"

sled   санки
'san-ki

(to) sleep   спать
spat(i)

small   маленький
'ma-l(i)en''-keėy

smile   улыбка
oo-'lyb-ka

snail   улитка
oo-'l(i)it-ka

snake   змея
zm(i)e-'ya

snow   снег
sn(i)eg

sock   чулок
choo-'lok

sofa   диван
d(i)i-'van

sparrow   воробей
vo-ro-'b(i)ey

spider   паук
pa-'ook

spiderweb   паутина
pa-oo-'t(i)i-na

spoon   ложка
'lozh-ka

squirrel   белка
'bel-ka

stairs   ступеньки
stoo-'pen''-kee

stamp   марка
'maar-ka

starfish   морская звезда
mor-'ska'-ya zv(i)iez-'da

stork   аист
'aa-eest

stove   плита
'plee-ta

strawberry   клубника
kloob-'n(i)i-ka

subway　　　метро
met-'ro

sugar cube　　сахар
'sa-khar

sun　　　солнце
sonn-tse

sunflower　　подсолнух
pod-'sol-nookh

sweater　　свитер
'sv(i)i-t(i)er

(to) sweep　　подметать
pod-m(i)e-'tat"

swing　　качели
ka-'che-l(i)i

table   стол
stohl

teapot   чайник
'chay-n(i)ik

teddy bear   мишка
'm(i)ish-ka

television   телевизор
te-le-'vi-zor

ten   десять
'd(i)e-s(i)at"

tent   палатка
pa-'lat-ka

theater театр
t(i)e-'atr

thimble напёрсток
na-'p(i)or-stok

(to) think думать
'doo-mat"

three три
tr(i)i

tie галстук
'gal-stook

(to) tie завязывать
za-'v(i)a'-zy-vat"

tiger тигр
t(i)igr

toaster тостер
'tos-ter

tomato помидор
po-mi-'dor

toucan тукан
too-'kan

towel полотенце
po-lo-'t(i)en-tse

tower башня
'bash-n(i)a

Tt

toy box   коробка для игрушек
ko-'rob-ka dl(i)a ig-'roo-shek

tracks   рельсы
'r(i)el"-sy

train station   станция
'staan-tsiya

tray   поднос
pod-'nos

tree   дерево
d(i)e-r(i)e-vo

trough   корыто
ko-'ry-to

truck

грузовик
groo-zo-'vik

trumpet   труба
troo-'ba

tulip   тюльпан
t(i)ul"-'pan

tunnel   туннель
too-'nehl"

turtle   черепаха
che-r(i)e-'paa-kha

twins   близнецы
bl(i)iz-n(i)e-tsy

two   два
dva

umbrella   зонтик
'zontik

uphill   в гору
v'go-roo

Vv

vase   ваза
'vaa-za

veil   вуаль
voo-'al"

village

деревня
d(i)e-r(i)ev-n(i)a

violet

фиалка
fee-'al-ka

violin

скрипка
'skr(i)ip-ka

voyage

путешествие
poo-t(i)e-'shest-vi-ye

waiter   официант
o-fi-tsi-'aant

(to) wake up   проснуться
pro-snoot-s(i)a

walrus   морж
morzh

(to) wash   стирать
st(i)i-'rat"

watch   часы
cha-'sy

(to) watch   наблюдать
na-bl(i)u-'dat"

(to) water поливать
po-l(i)i-'vat"

waterfall водопад
vo-do-'paad

watering can лейка
'l(i)ey-ka

watermelon арбуз
ar-'booz

weather vane флюгер
'fl(i)oo-ger

(to) weigh взвешивать
'vz-v(i)e-shi-vat"

whale кит
keet

wheel колесо
ko-l(i)e-'soh

wheelbarrow тачка
'taach-ka

whiskers усы
'oo-sy

(to) whisper шептать
shep-'tat"

whistle свисток
svis-'tok

white   **белый**
'b(i)e-ly

wig   **парик**
paa-'r(i)ik

wind   **ветер**
v(i)e-t(i)er

window   **окно**
ok-'noh

wings   **крылья**
kryl"-'ya

winter   **зима**
z(i)i-'maa

wolf   волк
                                            volk

wood   дрова   **word**   слово
                     dro-'va   *'sloh-voh*

(to) write   писать
                                            p(i)i-'sat"

yellow

желтый
'zhol-ty

zebra

зебра
'z(i)e-braa

Ё

ёж	hedgehog
ёлка	Christmas tree

Ж

желтый	yellow
жираф	giraffe
жокей	jockey
жонглёр	juggler
жук	beetle
журнал	magazine

З

забор	fence
завтрак	breakfast
завязывать	(to) tie
замок	castle
замок	lock
замок	padlock
занавеска	curtain
заплата	patch
звонить	(to) ring
зебра	zebra
зелёный	green
зеркало	mirror
зима	winter
змея	snake
золотая рыбка	goldfish
зонтик	umbrella

И

игла	needle
играть	(to) play
игрушечный домик	dollhouse
игрушка	toy
инструмент	instrument

ирис	iris
исследовать	(to) explore

К

кактус	cactus
канарейка	lovebird
канат	rope
капитан	captain
капуста	cabbage
карандаш	pencil
карета	coach
карта	map
карта	card
картофель	potato
кастрюля	pot
кататься на коньках	ice-skating
качели	swing
кафэ	café
кенгуру	kangaroo
кит	whale
клевать	(to) peck
клоун	clown
клубника	strawberry
ключ	key
книга	book
коала	koala bear
ковёр	carpet
коза	goat
кокос	coconut
колесо	wheel
колокол	bell
колыбель	cradle
кольцо	ring
компас	compass
конверт	envelope
конура	doghouse
конфета	candy
конь	horse
корабль	ship

корень	root
коричневый	brown
корзинка	basket
кормить	(to) feed
коробка для игрушек	toy box
корова	cow
королева	queen
корона	crown
корыто	trough
косилка	lawn mower
косточка	pit
кость	bone
котёнок	kitten
кошка	cat
краска	paint
красный	red
кровать	bed
кролик	rabbit
крылья	wings
крыша	roof
кубики	blocks
кубики льда	ice cubes
кувшин	pitcher
кузнечик	grasshopper
кукла	doll
кукуруза	corn
кулак	fist
курица	hen

Л

лаванда	lavender
лазить	(to) climb
лакать	(to) lap
лампа	lamp
лампочка	lightbulb
лев	lion
лейка	watering can
лесоруб	lumberjack

музыка	music
мышь	mouse
мяч	ball

Н

наблюдать	(to) watch
надувной плот	raft
наливать	(to) pour
напёрсток	thimble
нести	(to) carry
нога	leg, foot
нож	knife
ножницы	scissors
носорог	rhinoceros

О

обед	lunch
обезьяна	monkey
облако	cloud
обнимать	(to) hug
овца	sheep
огонь	fire
огурец	cucumber
одеяло	comforter
один	one
одуванчик	dandelion
океанский лайнер	ocean liner
окно	window
олень	deer
оленьи рога	antlers
омар	lobster
орёл	eagle
орех	nut
осёл	donkey
осень	autumn
остров	island
отвёртка	screwdriver
отец	father
открыто	open
официант	waiter
очки	glasses

лестница	ladder
летать	(to) fly
летучая мышь	bat
лимон	lemon
линейка	ruler
лиса	fox
лист	leaf
лицо	face
лодка	boat
ложка	spoon
локоть	elbow
лопата	shovel
лук	onion
луна	moon
люди	people
лягушка	frog

М

магнит	magnet
маленький	small
малина	raspberry
мальчик	boy
маринованый огурец	pickle
марка	stamp
маска	mask
матрос	sailor
мать	mother
маяк	lighthouse
мебель	furniture
мёд	honey
медведь	bear
метла	broom
метро	subway
миска	bowl
мишка	teddy bear
младенец	baby
молоток	hammer
молочник	milkman
морж	walrus
морковь	carrot
мороженое	ice cream
морская звезда	starfish
мост	bridge

П

палатка	tent
палец	finger
пальма	palm tree
пальто	coat
папоротник	fern
парашют	parachute
парик	wig
парк	park
парник	greenhouse
паровоз	engine
парта	desk
паспорт	passport
пастух	shepherd
паук	spider
паутина	spiderweb
пекарь	baker
пеликан	pelican
переходить	(to) cross
перо	feather
персик	peach
перчатка	glove
песочные часы	hourglass
петух	rooster
петь	(to) sing
печенье	cracker
пещера	cave
пианино	piano
пиджак	jacket

пижама	pajamas
пингвин	penguin
пирог	pie
писать	(to) write
пить	(to) drink
плакать	(to) cry
платочек	handkerchief
платье	dress
плита	stove
пляж	beach
подарок	present
подкова	horseshoe
подметать	(to) sweep
поднос	tray
подсолнух	sunflower
подушка	pillow
пожарная колонка	hydrant
показывать	(to) show
поле	field
полевая мышь	field mouse
ползать	(to) crawl
поливать	(to) water
полотенце	towel
помидор	tomato
пони	pony
попугай	parrot
пояс	belt
пробка	cork
проснутся	(to) wake up
прятаться	(to) hide
птица	bird
пустой	empty
пустыня	desert
путешествие	voyage
пчела	bee
пять	five

Р

радио	radio
радуга	rainbow
ракета	rocket
ракетка	racket
ракушка	shell
рамка	frame
расчёска	comb
редиска	radish
река	river
рельсы	tracks
рисовать	(to) draw
рога	horns
роза	rose
рот	mouth
рубашка	shirt
рука	hand
рукавица	mitten
рыба	fish
рысь	lynx
рыцарь	knight
рынок	marketplace
рюкзак	backpack

С

сад	garden
салат	lettuce
санки	sled
сапог	boot
самолёт	airplane
сахар	sugar cube
свечка	candle
свинья	pig

свисток	whistle
свитер	sweater
семь	seven
сено	hay
сердце	heart
сидеть	(to) sit
синий	blue
сирень	lilac
сито	sieve
скакать	(to) jump
скамья	bench
складная картинка	jigsaw puzzle
скрипка	violin
слива	plum
слово	word
слон	elephant
слушать	(to) listen
смех	laughter
снег	snow
собака	dog
собирать	(to) gather
сова	owl
солнце	sun
соловей	nightingale
соль	salt
сосна	pine
спать	(to) sleep
"Спокойной ночи"	"Good night"
ставень	shutter
стакан	glass
станция	train station
старый	old
стирать	(to) wash
стол	table
стрекоза	dragonfly
страус	ostrich
страх	fear

флюгер	weather vane
фокусник	magician
фонарик	flashlight
фонтан	fountain
фотоаппарат	camera
фрукты	fruit

Х

ходить под парусом	(to) sail
хлеб	bread
холодильник	refrigerator
хомяк	hamster
художник	painter

Ц

цвет	blossom
цветок	flower
цирк	circus

Ч

чайка	seagull
чайник	teapot
часы	watch
черепаха	turtle
черешня	cherry
чёрный	black
четыре	four
число	date
число	number
чистить	(to) peel
читать	(to) read
чулок	sock

Ш

шапка	cap
шарф	scarf
шептать	(to) whisper
шесть	six
шить	(to) sew
школа	school
шляпа	hat
шмель	bumblebee
шоколад	chocolate
шоссе	highway

Щ

щенок	puppy
щётка	brush

Э

эскалатор	escalator
эскимос	Eskimo

Я

яблоко	apple
яйцо	egg
ячмень	barley

стрела	arrow
стул	chair
ступеньки	stairs
сумка	handbag
сыр	cheese

Т

тачка	wheelbarrow
такси	cab
танцевать	(to) dance
тарелка	plate
театр	theater
телевизор	television
тетрадь	notebook
тигр	tiger
торт	cake
тостер	toaster
три	three
труба	chimney
труба	trumpet
тукан	toucan
туннель	tunnel
тыква	pumpkin
тюльпан	tulip
тянуть	(to) pull

У

удить	fish
узел	knot
улитка	snail
улыбка	smile
урожай	harvest
усы	whiskers
утка	duck
утконос	platypus
утюг	iron

Ф

фиалка	violet
флаг	flag

Folk Tales from Bohemia

Adolf Wenig

This folk tale collection is one of a kind, focusing uniquely on humankind's struggle with evil in the world. Delicately ornate red and black text and illustrations set the mood.

Ages 9 and up

90 pages • red and black illustrations • 5 1/2 x 8 1/4 • 0-7818-0718-2 • W • $14.95hc • (786)

Czech, Moravian and Slovak Fairy Tales

Parker Fillmore

Fifteen different classic, regional folk tales and 23 charming illustrations whisk the reader to places of romance, deception, royalty, and magic.

Ages 12 and up

243 pages • 23 b/w illustrations • 5 1/2 x 8 1/4 • 0-7818-0714-X • W • $14.95 hc • (792)

Glass Mountain: Twenty-Eight Ancient Polish Folk Tales and Fables

W.S. Kuniczak

Illustrated by Pat Bargielski

As a child in a far-away misty corner of Volhynia, W.S. Kuniczak was carried away to an extraordinary world of magic and illusion by the folk tales of his Polish nurse.

171 pages • 6 x 9 • 8 illustrations • 0-7818-0552-X • W • $16.95hc • (645)

Old Polish Legends

Retold by F.C. Anstruther

Wood engravings by J. Sekalski

This fine collection of eleven fairy tales, with an introduction by Zymunt Nowakowski, was first published in Scotland during World War II.

66 pages • 7 1/4 x 9 • 11 woodcut engravings • 0-7818-0521-X • W • $11.95hc • (653)

Folk Tales from Russia

by Donald A. Mackenzie

With nearly 200 pages and 8 full-page black-and-white illustrations, the reader will be charmed by these legendary folk tales that symbolically weave magical fantasy with the historic events of Russia's past.

Ages 12 and up

192 pages • 8 b/w illustrations • 5 1/2 x 8 1/4 • 0-7818-0696-8 • W • $12.50hc • (788)

Fairy Gold: A Book of Classic English Fairy Tales

Chosen by Ernest Rhys

Illustrated by Herbert Cole

Forty-nine imaginative black and white illustrations accompany thirty classic tales, including such beloved stories as "Jack and the Bean Stalk" and "The Three Bears."

Ages 12 and up

236 pages • 5 1/2 x 8 1/4 • 49 b/w illustrations • 0-7818-0700-X • W • $14.95hc • (790)

Tales of Languedoc: From the South of France

Samuel Jacques Brun

For readers of all ages, here is a masterful collection of folk tales from the south of France.

Ages 12 and up

248 pages • 33 b/w sketches • 5 1/2 x 8 1/4 • 0-7818-0715-8 • W • $14.95hc • (793)

Twenty Scottish Tales and Legends

Edited by Cyril Swinson

Illustrated by Allan Stewart

Twenty enchanting stories take the reader to an extraordinary world of magic harps, angry giants, mysterious spells and gallant Knights.

Ages 9 and up

215 pages • 5 1/2 x 8 1/4 • 8 b/w illustrations • 0-7818-0701-8 • W • $14.95 hc • (789)

Swedish Fairy Tales

Translated by H. L. Braekstad

A unique blending of enchantment, adventure, comedy, and romance make this collection of Swedish fairy tales a must-have for any library.

Ages 9 and up

190 pages • 21 b/w illustrations • 51/2 x 81/4 • 0-7818-0717-4 • W • $12.50hc • (787)

The Little Mermaid and Other Tales

Hans Christian Andersen

Here is a near replica of the first American edition of 27 classic fairy tales from the masterful Hans Christian Andersen.

Ages 9 and up

508 pages • b/w illustrations • 6 x 9 • 0-7818-0720-4 • W • $19.95hc • (791)

Pakistani Folk Tales: Toontoony Pie and Other Stories

Ashraf Siddiqui and Marilyn Lerch

Illustrated by Jan Fairservis

In these 22 folk tales are found not only the familiar figures of folklore—kings and beautiful princesses—but the magic of the Far East, cunning jackals, and wise holy men.

Ages 7 and up

158 pages • 6 1/2 x 8 1/2 • 38 illustrations • 0-7818-0703-4 • W • $12.50hc • (784)

Folk Tales from Chile

Brenda Hughes

This selection of 15 tales gives a taste of the variety of Chile's rich folklore. Fifteen charming illustrations accompany the text.

Ages 7 and up

121 pages • 5 1/2 x 8 1/4 • 15 illustrations • 0-7818-0712-3 • W • $12.50hc • (785)

All prices subject to change. **To purchase Hippocrene Books** contact your local bookstore, call (718) 454-2366, or write to: HIPPOCRENE BOOKS, 171 Madison Avenue, New York, NY 10016. Please enclose check or money order, adding $5.00 shipping (UPS) for the first book and $.50 for each additional book.